the Mold Code Handbook

the Mold Code Handbook

Expecting Moms and Children with Asthma Edition

MIDWEST AEROBIOLOGY LABS

iUniverse, Inc.
Bloomington

the Mold Code Handbook
Expecting Moms and Children with Asthma Edition

Midwest Aerobiology Labs
Crest Hill Illinois U.S.A

This Publication is designed to provide accurate and authoritative information in regard to the subject matter covered. It is sold with the understanding that the publisher is not engaged in rendering legal or other professional services. If legal advice or other expert assistance is required, the services of a competent professional person should be sought.

iUniverse books may be ordered through booksellers or by contacting:

iUniverse
1663 Liberty Drive
Bloomington, IN 47403
www.iuniverse.com
1-800-Authors (1-800-288-4677)

ISBN: 978-1-4759-6058-7 (sc)
ISBN: 978-1-4759-6059-4 (ebk)

Printed in the United States of America

iUniverse rev. date: 12/05/2012

Contents

Introduction

A recent study performed by a team of physicians and scientists from the University of Cincinnati, the Environmental Protection Agency (EPA), and the Cincinnati Children's Hospital has deduced that there are, in fact, three molds that are specifically linked to the development of childhood asthma:

1. **Aspergillus ochraceus**
2. **Aspergillius unguis; and**
3. **Penicillum variabile.**

These findings are important because according to the United States Environmental Protection Agency (US EPA), asthma afflicts approximately 9% of school-aged children. And, direct medical costs of asthma are nearly $15 billion yearly, with **several thousand deaths** and millions of lost work and school days.

This cohort study suggests that exposure during infancy is linked to these three mold species that are common to water-damaged buildings. The study demonstrated that these molds were later associated with childhood asthma at the age of seven.

This is further significant because until now there has been a lack of quantitative, standardized methods to determine if a home indoor environment is sufficiently benign, not posing any serious health risks to future occupants.

Enter DNA-based technology. Clinical studies prove that DNA-based technology can be successfully used to identify and quantify molds common to water-damaged buildings. This brand new technology opens up the door to standardization for mold testing and mold inspections.

Mold—The good, the bad and the ugly

First, let's define exactly what mold is. Molds are forms of fungi that occur naturally in the environment. They are in the earth and play an important role outdoors when it comes to breaking down matter such as plant debris. (More benefits can be read below.) In order for mold to reproduce, it makes tiny spores—just like some plants produce seeds. When indoors, mold spores move throughout the air and settle on various surfaces.

Typically, molds need moisture and food sources such as cloth, wood, drywall, etc. to grow. Now, mold may become troublesome if a wet surface is not dried up or promptly discarded. In fact, it will quickly grow within 24 to 48 hours. So, while mold is important in many ways, it also has some drawbacks. We need to be aware of these drawbacks and understand how to deal with them.

What Would Happen Without Mold?

- We would find ourselves walking waist-deep in dead plant matter.
- We wouldn't have great foods and certain kinds of cheese (mold is added for flavor).
- Medicine such as penicillin or any medicine name that ends in "mycin" would not exist.
- Meat would not be well preserved because butchers inject mold into animals before they butcher it to preserve the animal.
- We would not have beer or bread.
- Molds have many industrial uses such as in the fermentation of organic acids and cheeses.
- Some fungi, such as mushrooms and truffles, are tasty delicacies that enhance a wide variety of recipes, including pizza. These recipes would disappear.

What's all the fuss about mold?

While in nature, mold plays a key role. However, problems arise when mold starts digesting organic materials that we don't want them to (e.g., our homes and agricultural crops).

Mold: The Master of Reproduction

Mold is a reproduction master. In the common bread mold, Rhizopus stolonifer, the tiny black dots are the spore bodies, or sporangia. Just one dot contains upwards of 50,000 spores, each of which can produce hundreds of millions of new spores in a matter of days! (Awake, 2006) One specimen of the common group fungus, Ganoderma applanatum, can discharge 30,000,000,000 spores a day, every day, from the beginning of May through September (4,500,000,000,000 spores).

Mold spores are dispersed in the vastness of the atmosphere. So, where do these mold spores go? Everywhere! Mold spores are transported globally in clouds of atmospheric dust.

Many species of mold — including some that are human pathogens — have characteristics suited for long-range atmospheric transport; they can be distributed evenly throughout the earth's atmosphere.

For example: Mold spores from Africa can affect not only the air quality in Africa, but also in Europe, the Middle East, and the United States. Subsequently, mold spores found in Asia, affect not only the air quality in Asia, but also in the Arctic, North America, and Europe.

Additionally, mold spores within these atmospheric dust clouds may affect human health directly or indirectly through downwind ecosystems in both outdoor and indoor environments. Remember, all that's needed for mold to survive is moisture, oxygen, and something to feed on.

How Mold Affects the Human Body

On the following pages, we have attempted to categorize several common species of mold.

Molds That Cause Asthma

A recent study performed by a team of physicians and scientists from the University of Cincinnati, the Environmental Protection Agency (EPA), and the Cincinnati Children's Hospital has deduced that there are, in fact, three molds that are specifically linked to the development of childhood asthma:

- ✓ **Aspergillus ochraceus**
- ✓ **Aspergillius unguis; and**
- ✓ **Penicillum variabile.**

Potentially Opportunistic or Infectious Molds

Opportunistic and infectious mold are molds that take advantage of certain opportunities to cause disease. These opportunities are called "opportunistic conditions." These molds are often ones that can lie dormant in body tissues for many years (e.g., the human herpes virus), or that are extremely common, but usually cause no symptoms of illness. When the immune system cannot raise an adequate response, these microorganisms are activated, begin to multiply, and soon overwhelm the body's weakened defenses.

Here is a list of molds known to be "opportunistic" or "infectious" and that have been isolated in infestations causing adverse health effects:

- Acremonium spp.
- Aspergillus spp.
- Bipolaris
- Candida spp.
- Curvularia
- Exserohilum
- Fusarium spp.
- Paecilomyces spp.
- Penicillium spp.
- Rhizopus spp.
- Scedosporium spp.
- Scopulariopsis brevicaulis
- Trichoderma

The following human diseases could potentially be associated with the above mold species:

Superficial Candidosis (candidiasis): An acute or chronic invasive infection in an immunocompromised individual. It also causes mucosal, cutaneous or nail infection.

Keratomycosis (mycotic keratitis): A fungal infection of the cornea. This infection is difficult to treat and can cause severe visual impairment or blindness.

Otomycosis: A superficial fungal infection of the ear canal.

Aspergillosis: In immunocompromised individuals, inhalation of Aspergillius spores can result in life-threatening, invasive infection of the lungs or sinuses. In non-immunocompromised persons, these molds can cause localized infection of the lungs, sinuses and other organs. Inhalation of Aspergillius spores can also cause allergic symptoms.

Mucormycosis (zygomycosis): This can cause rhinocerebral, pulmonary, gastrointestinal, cutaneous or disseminated infection in predisposed individuals.

Other Symptoms of Infectious Molds

Fungal ball: A condition where the fungus actively proliferates in the human lung, forming a ball.

Potentially "Toxic" Mold

Journalists have used the term "toxic mold" when writing about molds that have been implicated in severe health reactions in humans or highly-publicized court cases.

However, the term "toxic" mold is somewhat misleading because it implies the idea that certain **molds** are toxic, when in fact **all** molds are capable of producing **secondary substances** or metabolites that produce toxins.

The correct terminology is called mycotoxins or in layman's terms—**potentially** toxigenic molds—putting the emphasis on "potentially." Under certain growth and environmental conditions these molds are capable of eliciting a negative health response in humans and animals.

Although a specific mold might have the potential to produce mycotoxins, it will not produce them if the appropriate environmental conditions do not exist. Currently, the specific conditions that cause mycotoxin production are not fully understood.

Here is a list of molds known to potentially produce mycotoxins and which have been isolated in infestations causing adverse health effects:

- Acremonium spp.
- Alternaria spp.
- Aspergillus spp.
- Chaetomium spp.
- Cladosporium spp.
- Fusarium spp.
- Paecilomyces
- Penicillium spp.
- Stachybotrys spp.
- Trichoderma spp.

The following human disease could potentially be associated with the above mold species.

- Mycotoxicosis—poisoning due to a fungal bi-product (Mycotoxin). Ingestion of some mycotoxins can cause liver cancer. There is also some evidence that inhalation of certain toxins can cause lung cancer.

Other Symptoms of "Mycotoxicosis"

These include: allergic reactions, rhinitis and dermatitis, nausea, vomiting, dermatitis, diarrhea and upset stomach, extensive internal bleeding, hemorrhagic syndrome (alimentary toxic aleukia), acute gastrointestinal illness, mucous membrane irritation, skin rash, immune system suppression, acute or chronic liver damage, acute or chronic central nervous system damage, and others.

Molds Associated With Water-Damaged Buildings

The below list of molds is common in the following circumstances: Basement water intrusion; chronic relative humidity; damage coolant line insulation; damp crawlspace; excessive moisture in the HVAC; flooding; foreclosure or vacant property; ice damming issues; moisture intrusion; sump pumps failure; sewer back-up; stagnant water; water damaged carpet, fabric and compromised construction material.

- Aspergillus flavus
- Aspergillus fumigatus
- Aspergillus niger
- Aspergillus ochraceus
- Aspergillus penicilloides
- Aspergillus restrictus
- Aspergillus sclerotiorum
- Aspergillus sydowii
- Aspergillus unguis
- Aspergillus veriscolor
- Aureobasidium
- Chaetomium globosum
- Cladosporium sphaerospermum
- Eurotium amstelodami
- Paecilomyces
- Penicillium brevicompactum
- Penicillium corylophilum
- Penicillium crustosum
- Penicillium purpurogenum
- Penicillium spinulosum
- Penicillium variabile
- Scopulariopsis
- Scopulariopsis brevicaulis
- Stachybotrys chartarum
- Trichoderma viride
- Wallemia sebi

Leaf—Surface Fungi

The types of surface fungi listed below are common in homes, even without water damage. These molds come from outdoor sources (e.g., growth on leaf surfaces). Although indoor sources are possible, they are not common in indoor mold infestation. Presence in indoor air generally reflects outside air ventilation (blown in from the outside); windows, doors, etc.

- Acremonium strictum
- Alternaria alternata
- Aspergillus ustus
- Cladosporium cladosporioides
- Cladosporium herbarum
- Epicoccum nigrum
- Mucor racemosus
- Penicillium chrysogenum
- Rhizopus stolonifer

NOTE: Please keep in mind that all of the preceding lists are not all-inclusive. With more than 100,000 species in the world, research is ongoing.

Hoarding and Mold: A Deadly Combination

Mold levels in a hoarder's home can be extremely high causing recurring infections, repeated hospitalization and even death.

Moderate to severe hoarding is associated with mold growth. Elevated mold spores are often found in a hoarder's home which can cause respiratory problems, hospitalization and even death. Therefore, the elderly and especially people with immunodeficiency conditions MUST REFRAIN FROM HOARDING!

Often, a home with **excessive contents** and clutter will experience a restriction in air circulation, sustained humidity and other circumstances that discourage the natural dehumidification that takes place in a home.

To make matters worse, when the operation of the heating, ventilation and air conditioning (HVAC) system is limited or if the HVAC system is completely turned off, the interior space of the home will become **damp**, often attaining conditions near the **dew point** (100% Relative Humidity).

This is where the nightmare begins; excessive clutter will absorb this moisture and create the ideal breeding ground for mold.

Mold investigations made difficult

Homes containing excessive contents pose a concern because moisture and mold problems can be obscured and physically difficult to find. In addition, navigating around the excessive contents and clutter is challenging. Investigative methods using visual clues, flashlights, moisture meters and infrared cameras are rendered ineffective when potentially-damaged floors and walls are inaccessible.

What should you do?

Completely eliminate or reduce excessive contents or clutter. Of course this is more easily said than done; professional help will likely be necessary. Consider hiring a hoarding cleanup firm.

NOTE: Hoarding cleanup is a specialized field and the service goes well beyond junk hauling or basic cleaning. These companies specialize in "hoarding" clean up and can provide other invaluable services such as:

- Psychologists/Psychiatrists
- Free Phone and E-mail Support (for any of your questions)
- Hoarding and Clutter Clean up
- Sorting of Contents
- Recovery of Valuables and Sentimental Items
- Paperwork Recovery and Storage
- Cleanup and Disposal of Animal and/or Human Waste
- Appliance Recycling
- E-Waste Recycling
- Delivery of Storage Containers
- Removal and Recycling of Non Running Vehicles
- Photo/Video Documentation
- Itemized Inventory
- Deep Cleaning
- Home Repairs—Paint, Drywall, Carpet, Electrical, Plumbing, Etc.
- Additional Follow Up Care (home visits, meals, weekly cleaning/ maintenance, therapists)

Other recommendations

Keep garages, basements and crawlspaces clean and free of excessive contents and clutter.

The natural airflow of your home is from the ground up through the roof. As a result, the air you breathe upstairs originates from the basement or crawl space and the lower levels of the house. Therefore, it is critical to especially keep these areas clean and free from clutter that can easily get trapped and create moisture and mold.

By eliminating excessive contents and clutter, you will reduce the mold problem and ultimately improve your indoor air quality.

Developing an Enforceable Mold Testing Standard Based on DNA Technology—Is it Possible?

The answer is yes! There are several components necessary to establish a standard for mold testing. They include:

1. The scientific basis for the standard
2. A standardized sampling strategy
3. A standardized, field sampling, laboratory and analytical methods

Linking the necessary components to mold exposure limits would require identifying the highest concentration of a specific mold species.

Example 1: Mold species such as Aspergillus ochraceus, Aspergillius unguis or Penicillum variabile have been well documented to affect infants, often leading to an increased chance of childhood asthma.

Example 2: People who are immunocompromised and are repeatedly exposed to infectious mold species such as Candida spp. or Aspergillus spp. in the home/office could prove detrimental to their health.
As you can see, it is critical that mold assessments are accurate and meaningful. And, only a DNA-based technology can satisfy these demanding components by employing real DNA science. Benefits of DNA-based mold analysis include:

- A 99.99% accuracy rate; there is no human error!
- Spore fragment detection that provides the exact number of spores in each sample
- Identification of actual mold species found (e.g., DNA differentiates Aspergillus from Penicillium)

5
Developing an Indoor Benign Environment Ordinance

NOTE: The EPA does not regulate mold or mold spores in indoor air. It is, however, permissible for local government (municipalities) to adopt local mold-testing standards and ordinances that would allow for ENFORCEABLE Mold Investigations. Doing so, would provide Code enforcers with the opportunity to determine if an indoor environment is sufficiently benign, and does not pose any serious health risks to themselves, current or future occupants.

Once the indoor environment meets healthy home's standards then the building owner receives the Indoor Benign Environment ™ (IBE) Certificate.

So, adopting an IBE ordinance is an important consideration. Let's take a look below at what such an ordinance would look like:

<u>Example</u>: Indoor Benign Environment ™ (IBE) Ordinance

During the transfer of property in real estate disclosure statements, and prior to a prospective tenant entering into a contract/lease, the IBE Ordinance requires that the presence of indoor mold and its levels be disclosed.

Such an ordinance is useful because it helps to identify homes and work places that have suffered water damage, but do not display easily identifiable signs. It is recommended that municipalities adopt the IBE ordinance to determine if a home or workplace may place asthma or immunocompromised individuals at greater risk for adverse health effects.

Once adopted by the municipality, enforcement of the standards could be performed by any of the following:

    a. Public health officers
    b. Code enforcement officers
    c. Environmental health officers
    d. City attorneys
    e. Any other appropriate government entities

These same entities may respond to complaints about mold and enforce any standards adopted by the municipality and/or the disclosure requirements of this Code.

Mold Guidelines

It is important to determine if an indoor environment is sufficiently benign, and does not pose any serious health risk.

This part of the publication is divided into paragraphs, each pertaining to a mold-related subject. Each paragraph is numbered; therefore, paragraphs are referred to by mold-related subject and paragraph number. All cross-references are by paragraph notation.

Mold Guidelines—*Quick Reference Guide*

LICENSING OR REGISTRATION

Licensing or Registration

1. Municipality licensing or registration is required for any mold-related work or any work related to indoor environmental inspections and testing, mold assessment, mold testing, mold analysis, mold evaluation, mold inspection, mold sampling, mold consulting, mold remediation, mold removal, mold cleanup, removal of stagnant water and/or disinfection.
2. Any person, firm or corporation engaged in any form of mold-related activity, before undertaking such activity, shall first license or register the name and address of such a person, firm or corporation with the municipality.

Registration or Licensing—Exceptions

3. The following persons are not required to comply with any provisions of this Code relating to registration and licensing:

   - An authorized employee of the United States, this state, or any municipality, county, or other political subdivision, or public or private school who is conducting mold assessment within the scope of that employment, as long as the employee does not hold out for hire to the general public or otherwise engage in any mold-related activity.
   - An employee of an insurance company or an insurance adjuster, when the employee or insurance adjuster is adjusting a claim under an insurance policy.

Renewal

4. A person shall not perform **any** mold-related activity with an expired license or registration.

Reinstatement—Licensing or Registration

5. Any person, firm or corporation that shall be convicted under this Code and shall have his name removed from such licensing or registration may have same name reinstated upon filing with the Building Commissioner or president of the municipality to the effect that all ordinance violations have been corrected or are nonexistent and that all claims and judgments arising from such convictions have been paid.

6. Additionally, a new licensing or registration may be required, along with the appropriate fees established by the municipality.

Noncompliance, Revocation

7. The municipality may revoke a license or registration of any person, firm or corporation who:

   - Has expired insurance
   - Fails to register **all** mold remediation employees
   - Fails to obtain a permit required pursuant to provisions of this Code relating to mold remediation, mold removal, and disinfection after mold removal of any building or part thereof
   - Obtains a permit, but performs work not in compliance with the terms of the permit or in violation of the provisions of this Code
   - Performs work, whether a permit is required or obtained, and fails to comply with the mold remediation guidelines established by US EPA: "A Brief Guide To Mold, Moisture, And Your Home"—EPA 402-K-02-003 and "Mold Remediation in Schools and Commercial Buildings"—EPA 402-K-01-001
   - Has fraudulently or deceptively obtained or attempted to obtain the license or registration
   - Falsifies records that the municipality requires the mold inspector or mold remediator to submit
   - Is convicted of a felony or misdemeanor arising from a mold inspection and or remediation project

8. The municipality's building commissioner or president may request their corporate counsel to bring suit and prosecute the person or entity for such violations. Upon entry of a finding that a Code violation exists by an administrative law officer or a finding of guilty against such an owner or person(s) by a court of complete jurisdiction, the name of the person or entity shall be revoked from the municipality registration or license records and shall not be entered, reentered or reinstated during such time as any violation exists or any judgment remains unsatisfied with regard to a guilty finding.

Penalty

9. Any person, firm or corporation violating, resisting or opposing the enforcement of any of the provisions of this Code, where no other penalty is provided, shall be fined not less than $25, and no more than $200 **for each offense**. Each day such violation shall continue, shall constitute a separate and distinct offense; and any owner or contractor who shall perform any work in violation of the provisions of this Code, have supervision of such building, or who shall permit any work to be performed, shall be liable for the penalties imposed by this Code.

Conflict of Interest

10. Licensee or registrant shall not perform both mold inspection and mold remediation services on the same building project.
11. A licensee or registrant shall not own an interest in an entity that performs mold inspection services and an entity that performs mold remediation services on the same building project.

Insurance Requirements

12. Municipality is to be named as additional insured. Certificate must bear the endorsement that insurance may not be canceled by the insurer with at least twenty (20) days prior written notice to the municipality. Cancellation of such insurance will cause automatic revocation of the license or registration. (see figure 1)

(Figure 1)

Insurance Requirements

Commercial General Liability Coverage (For Remediation Contractors and Mold Inspectors)

Gen Aggregate Limit	$1,000,000
Each Occurrence Limit:	$1,000,000

Professional Liability Coverage (For Mold Inspectors Only)

Aggregate Limit	$1,000,000
Each Incident Limit	$1,000,000

Worker's Compensation Coverage (For Mold Remediation Contractors Only).

Each Accident	$100,000
Disease Policy Limit	$500,000
Each Employee	$100,000

Surety Bond (For Mold Remediation Contractors Only).

Signed Surety Bond $10,000

NOTE: Contractor shall provide the municipality with their insurance policy declaration page. The declaration page shall match the services and/or products offered.

PERMITS

Mold Remediation—Permit Required

13. It shall be unlawful to proceed with mold remediation, mold removal, mold cleanup, or any other mold-related activity without permits.

Permit Exceptions

14. The following persons listed below are not required to comply with any provisions of this part relating to registration:

   - A permit shall not be required for mold inspections (mold testing and sampling, etc.).
   - A remediation permit shall not be required if an area where the mold contamination for the total project affects a total surface area of less than 10 square feet. (See "A Brief Guide To Mold, Moisture, And Your Home"—EPA 402-K-02-003)
   - An authorized employee of the United States, this state, or any municipality, county, or other political subdivision, or public or private school and who is conducting mold assessment within the scope of that employment, as long as the employee does not hold out for hire to the general public or otherwise engage in mold assessment.

Notification of Mold Remediation and Notice of Mold Removal Completion

15. It is critical to assess the size of the mold and/or moisture problem and the type of damaged materials before planning the remediation work. The remediation should include steps to fix the water or moisture problem, or the problem may reoccur.

16. (See Mold Remediation guidelines established by US EPA: "A Brief Guide To Mold, Moisture, And Your Home"—EPA 402-K-02-003 and "Mold Remediation in Schools and Commercial Buildings"—EPA 402-K-01-001)

Notification of Mold Remediation (NMR) Form

17. A municipality-licensed mold remediator is required to submit an NMR form detailing the methods and procedures to complete the remediation project to the municipality for approval at least five working days in advance of the project.
18. The municipality will review the NMR form, request changes if necessary, and give the mold remediator permission to proceed.

Hidden Mold Found

19. If additional mold contamination is discovered during the remediation project, the municipality-licensed mold remediator is required to contact the municipality to have the NMR form reassessed.

Post-Remediation Verification Inspection

20. A Post-Remediation Verification Inspection shall be performed by a municipality-licensed mold inspector.
21. The purpose of the inspection is to verify that the remediation has been properly executed and that the area has been restored to what would be considered a benign indoor environment.
22. Where visual and/or olfactory inspections reveal deficiencies sufficient to fail clearance, EPA's DNA Mold Analysis need not be used.

Municipality Required Mold Inspections

23. The following real estate circumstances require a mold inspection by a municipality-licensed mold inspector:

    - Vacant Properties—prior to real estate closing or leasing
    - Vacant properties disconnected from the public water system
    - The sale of all foreclosed, vacant, and bank-owned properties located within the municipality
    - Remodeling and Rehabilitation Permits—Final Approval
    - Construction Permits—Final Occupancy

- New Construction Permits—Final Occupancy
- During routine building inspections when stagnant water or visible molds are discovered.

Affidavit Process

24. If the building fails the mold inspection, future building inspections WILL NOT be scheduled or performed, until the building is sufficiently benign and safe for Municipal Personnel to enter premises.
25. The seller and buyer **jointly** have two options;

- Seller remediates prior to real estate closing and performs a Post-Remediation Verification Inspection to verify that the indoor environment is sufficiently benign and safe for Municipal Personnel to enter premises.
- Seller and buyer agree to remediate after the real estate closing; a Mold Affidavit is signed by both the buyer and seller and cleared by the municipality to permit remediation and a Post-Remediation Verification after the property has transferred ownership.

Properties—Disconnected from the Public Water System

26. Properties that are deemed vacant become a nuisance and can be immediately disconnected from the public water system. The following steps shall take place:

- Vacant properties disconnected from the public water system shall not be reconnected until a mold inspection is performed by a municipality licensed or registered mold inspector.
- If the property fails the mold inspection, the water service will not be reconnected, until the building is sufficiently benign and safe for Municipal Personnel to enter premises.
- Mold inspections are good for 30 days from the date of the inspection.

Visible Mold

27. Visible mold in attic (underneath roof decking and roof joist); underneath sub-floor joist; Visible mold on construction materials such as drywall, wood studs, paneling, etc.

   - Mold shall not be allowed to colonize on ANY construction materials. The underlying moisture condition supporting mold growth shall be identified, and the following steps shall take place:
   - A municipality-licensed mold remediator is required to submit a Notification of Mold Remediation (NMR) form detailing methods and procedures to complete the remediation project to the municipality for approval at least five working days in advance of the project.
   - The municipality will review the NMR form, request changes if necessary, and give the mold remediator permission to proceed.
   - A Post-Remediation Verification Inspection shall be performed by a municipality licensed mold inspector.

28. The purpose of the inspection is to verify that the remediation has been properly executed and that the area has been restored to what would be considered a benign indoor environment.

Stagnant Water

Flooded Basements and Crawl Spaces

29. Every building, or part thereof, which is in an unsanitary condition because the basement or crawl space has been covered with stagnant water; there is presence of visible mold/fungi; any portion of a building has been infected with mold/fungi, or is unfit for human habitation; or has any other unsanitary condition, is a source of sickness, or, endangers the public health, is hereby declared to be a nuisance. The following steps shall take place:

- The owner of the building or the owner's agent shall be required to perform a mold inspection by a municipality licensed mold inspector and;
- Submit mold inspection results, along with a Notification of Mold Remediation (NMR) form to the municipality.

30. It shall be unlawful to proceed with mold remediation, mold removal, mold cleanup, removal of stagnant water or any other mold-related activity without permits.

Disposal of Stagnant Water

31. Disposal of moldy stagnant water draining from a crawl space or basement onto property or adjacent property shall not be permitted without the specific approval from the municipality. Any person, firm or corporation violating this Code shall be fined $200 for each offense.

Heating, Ventilation and Air Conditioning (HVAC)

32. Cleaning a building's air ducts generally refers to the cleaning of various heating and cooling system components of forced-air systems. These components may become contaminated with mold if moisture is present within the system, resulting in the potential release of mold spores throughout the building. Therefore, all components of the system must be cleaned. Failure to clean a component of a contaminated system may result in re-contamination of the entire system. Water-damaged or contaminated porous materials in the ductwork, or other air-handling system components, should be removed and replaced. Ventilation-system filters should be checked and replaced regularly to ensure that they are installed properly and should be replaced on a routine schedule. If an HVAC system is contaminated with mold, the following steps shall take place:

- The HVAC system shall be turned off
- Vents and ducts shall be covered

- Cleaning and disinfection of the entire HVAC system shall be required (supply vents and return air ducts)
- Any needed repairs or cleaning of vents and air ducts shall be performed before restarting the system; and wet or water-damaged filters shall be thrown away.

Mold Cleaning Procedures

33. Once the mold and moisture problem has been identified and corrected, physical extraction of mold and mold spores is critical. Simply encapsulating or painting over with primer is not acceptable.
34. Whether or not a specific type of mold is present shall not change the remediation method of removing or cleaning contaminated materials and a final surface HEPA vacuuming.
35. Furthermore, the absence of a specific type of mold known to cause health problems shall not be a rational basis for leaving visible mold growth un-remediated

If remediation is required, the following procedures shall take place:

- Only non-porous (e.g., metals, glass and hard plastics) and semi-porous (e.g., wood and concrete) materials that are structurally sound can be cleaned and reused
- Cleaning shall be completed using an appropriate cleaning agent
- All materials that will be reused shall be dry and visibly free from mold
- Porous materials such as ceiling tiles, insulation, and gypsum board shall not be cleaned and shall be removed and discarded as described in these guidelines
- The use of gaseous, vapor-phase or aerosolized biocides or odor suppressants for remedial purposes shall not permitted without specific approval from the municipality
- Building occupants should be temporarily relocated during the remediation project and personal protective equipment, including at minimum, gloves and eye protection shall be worn

- Contaminated materials that cannot be cleaned shall be removed from the building in a sealed plastic bag or wrapped and sealed in polyethylene sheeting and disposed of
- At the completion of the remediation project, all surfaces, including carpeting, in the vicinity of the remediation area shall be HEPA vacuumed and nonporous surfaces shall be damp wiped and the floors mopped with the appropriate cleaning agent
- All areas shall be left dry and visibly free from contamination and dust/debris
- Municipality may perform project oversight to include periodic inspections to ensure that the project is completed in compliance with the work plan and complete post-remediation verification.

36. A Post-Remediation Verification Inspection is required

Interpretation of DNA Mold Analysis and Environmental Survey Report

37. The ERMI is a screening tool developed by the US EPA to assist in predicting the relative "mold burden" on a given home. The ERMI was developed by screening dust samples from 1,096 homes across the United States as part of the 2006 HUD American Healthy Home Survey, and ranking these homes in an RMI (Relative Moldiness Index). The ERMI score is determined by analyzing dust samples by quantitative PCR for 36 species of mold divided into two groups. Group I is comprised of 26 species of molds commonly associated with water damage. Group II is comprised of 10 species of common to indoor environments. By comparing the difference in Group I and Group II molds, an ERMI score is generated which can then be compared to the nationwide RMI. (Forensic Analytical Laboratories 2012)

38. US EPA ERMI Mold DNA Analysis shall be performed by a municipality licensed or registered mold inspector; dust samples shall be analyzed using US EPA's—ERMI DNA Mold Protocol; and a home shall be given a score based on the Environmental Relative Moldiness Index (ERMI).

Interpretation of the Relative Moldiness Index (RMI) Score shall be as follows: (See figure 2)

Figure 2

ERMI Score	Level or Risk	Likelihood of Mold Problem in Home
-10 to -4	Level 1	Lowest
-4 to 0	Level 2	Lower
0 to 5	Level 3	Moderate
5 to 20	Level 4	High

39. If asthma causing molds such as Aspergillus ochraceus, Aspergillius unguis or Penicillum variabile are found at "moderate" to "high" levels, remediation shall take place and a Post-Remediation Verification inspection of the building shall be required to determine if remediation was successful.

40. Subsequently, if infectious molds are discovered, the municipality at its discretion may require remediation and a Post-Remediation Verification of the building to determine if remediation was successful.

Final Interpretation of Mold Inspection

41. The Environmental Survey Report (ESR) form shall be used in conjunction with the USEPA's Environmental Relative Moldiness Index (ERMI) score. Visual information and environmental conditions measured during the (ESR) assessment shall determine the **final** interpretation of (ERMI) results. (See Environmental Survey Report Form and Example ERMI DNA Analysis Report)

Schools and Commercial Buildings

42. Interpretation shall be conducted with caution. At present there are no environmental surveys for schools and commercial buildings to support the ERMI Score.

43. However, the **DNA Data** from the Mold DNA Analysis shall be used to document the identification of mold(s) and their measurements. This data will be useful to determine if an indoor environment is sufficiently benign, and does not pose any serious health risk.

44. If infectious molds are discovered, the municipality at its discretion may require remediation and a Post-ERMI DNA Mold Analysis.

Records

45. Records are needed for registered or licensed mold inspectors; mold remediators; and mold analysis laboratories. Records and documents required by this Code shall be retained for a period of three years from the date of the project's completion, unless otherwise stated. Upon demand, such records and documents shall be made available for inspection by the municipality.

46. **Records to be retained:**

- The name of each of its employees who worked on the project
- Contract between company and the customer (s)
- Copies of all laboratory results
- Copies of all photographs relating to remediation project
- Copies of all mold remediation and/or disinfection plans and any changes as a result of new discoveries; and copies of all clearance reports issued by the mold inspector

Mold Inspector's Qualifications and Certifications

In this chapter, we will discuss mold inspectors' qualifications and certification.

Mold Inspector Qualifications

1. Definition—A mold inspector is a person who has been licensed or registered by the municipality to perform mold inspections. A mold inspector's duties include: (a) an inspection, investigation, or survey of a dwelling or other structure to determine the presence of mold; (b) the development of a mold remediation and/or disinfection plan; and (c) the collection of a mold or dust samples to be analyzed.

Licensing or Registration

2. An individual must be licensed with the municipality as a mold inspector to perform activities listed under this Code.

Certifications

3. In addition to the requirements for all mold inspectors listed in this Code (relating to licensing or registration and insurance requirements), a mold inspector shall have at least one of the recognized certifications:

   - Industrial Hygienist
   - Healthy Homes Specialist (HHS)
   - Council-Certified Indoor Environmental Consultant (CIEC)

Scope of Inspection

4. Pre-Mold Inspections and Post-Remediation Verification Inspections

The following steps shall take place during a mold inspection:

a. A mold inspector shall determine the location and extent of mold or suspected mold present in an interior structure only
b. An infrared camera shall be used to identify potential moisture intrusion problems (windows, doors, skylights, ceiling lines, attic water intrusion, foundation moisture intrusion, pipe and condenser line leaks, etc.)

c. An Environmental Survey Report (ESR) shall be completed for each property inspected. Temperature and relative humidity during the initial mold inspection and/or post-remediation mold inspection shall be recorded (See ESR Form)

d. Mold inspector shall use only the US EPA Environmental Relative Moldiness Index (ERMI) for both Pre-Mold Inspection and Post-Remediation Verification

e. Mold inspector shall only use laboratories that are licensed by the US EPA to perform ERMI DNA Analysis.

5. Dust samples shall be collected from each property inspected and sampling shall be performed as follows:

a. Proper sample documentation shall be submitted, including the sample identification code; each location sampled; the date collected; the name of the mold inspector who collected the samples; and the project name and/or address shall be recorded for each sample, either on the sample itself or the chain of custody form

b. Collected dust samples must be prepped and analyzed by an EPA-approved laboratory or its agent that is licensed or registered under this Code

c. All dust samples shall be analyzed using the US EPA's ERMI Protocol.

6. Post-remediation verification inspection shall, to the extent possible, determine that the underlying cause of the mold has been remediated so that it is reasonably certain that the mold will not return from that remediated cause.

Fees

d. Pay the appropriate fees established by the municipality. Fees are based on a one-year license or registration.

Mold Remediators Qualifications and Certifications

In this chapter we will discuss mold remediators' qualifications and certification.

1. A mold remediator—is a person who is licensed by the municipality to perform mold remediation. His/Her duties include: cleaning mold from building material surfaces; removal of contaminated building materials that are unsalvageable; and applying disinfectants intended to prevent future mold contamination.

2. Additionally, the mold remediator shall provide the following duties:

   a. Mold remediation project oversight
   b. Appropriate training to employees that perform mold remediation
   c. Periodic reviews of the overall effectiveness of the mold remediation procedures and updates as required.

Licensing or Registration

3. An individual must be licensed or registered with the municipality as a mold remediator to perform activities listed under this Code.

Certifications

4. In addition to the requirements for all mold remediators listed in this Code (relating to licensing and/or registration and insurance requirements), a mold remediator shall have at least one of the following accredited certifications:

   - Industrial Hygienist
   - Healthy Homes Specialist (HHS)
   - Council-Certified Indoor Environmental Remediator (CIER)
   - Council-Certified Microbial Remediator (CMR)
   - Council-Certified Microbial Remediation Supervisor (CMRS)

Scope of work

5. An individual licensed under this section shall perform mold remediation and supervise registered mold remediation workers (helpers) performing mold remediation and/or disinfection services.
6. A licensed or registered mold remediation contractor shall follow a remediation and/or disinfection work plan providing instructions to their employees for the remediation efforts to be performed for a mold remediation project.
7. A licensed or registered mold remediator shall comply with the mold remediation guidelines established by US EPA guidelines: "A Brief Guide To Mold, Moisture, And Your Home"—EPA 402-K-02-003; and "Mold Remediation in Schools and Commercial Buildings"—EPA 402-K-01-001.

Mandatory Employee Training

8. All personnel involved with mold remediation shall receive training consistent with their duties. Employees will receive training to acquire the understanding, knowledge and skills necessary for the safe performance of the duties assigned under this program.
9. The training shall establish employee proficiency in the duties required and shall introduce new or revised procedures, as necessary, for compliance.

Training content shall include:

10. Methods and procedures for mold remediation to include:

    a. isolation of HVAC systems
    b. installation of isolation barriers and protection of non-contaminated materials within the remediation area
    c. remediation, cleaning and disposal of mold-contaminated materials
    d. final cleaning of remediation area
    e. personal protective equipment including OSHA Respiratory Protection Standard

Documentation

11. Training documentation shall be kept for all affected employees.

12. **NOTE**: All mold remediation employees shall register with the municipality under this Code.

Fees

13. Pay the appropriate fees established by the municipality. Fees are based on a one-year license or registration.

Mold Remediation Employees Qualifications and Certifications

In this chapter we will discuss mold remediation employees' qualifications.

Mold Remediation Employees

1. An individual licensed under this Code can perform mold remediation and/or disinfection services while supervised by a municipality-approved mold remediation contractor.

Licensing or Registration

2. An individual must be licensed or registered with the municipality as a mold remediation employee to perform activities listed under this Code.

Age Requirement

3. Each individual applying to be licensed or registered with the municipality as a mold remediation employee under this Code shall be at least 18 years old at the time of licensing or registration.

Scope of work

4. General containment setup, mold remediation and/or disinfection services.
5. **NOTE**: All employees shall be supervised by a municipality-licensed or registered mold remediator.

Protective Equipment Requirement

6. Mold remediation employees shall wear the following personal protective equipment (PPE) during the remediation process:

   a. A minimum of an N-95 respirator
   b. Gloves made from natural rubber, neoprene, nitrile, polyurethane, or PVC
   c. Safety glasses or goggles

Fees

7. Pay the appropriate fees established by the municipality. Fees are based on a one-year license or registration.
8. **NOTE**: Using professional judgment, a municipality-licensed or registered mold remediation contractor may specify additional or more protective PPE if he/she determines that it is warranted.

Mold Analysis Laboratory Qualifications and Certification

In this chapter we will discuss mold analysis laboratory qualifications and certification.

Qualifications

1. A mold laboratory and/or its agent shall be licensed or registered to engage in activities listed under this Code.

Scope of Work

2. Authorized to analyze samples collected during a mold inspection to:

   a. Implement USEPA ERMI Testing Protocol
   b. If applicable, provide onsite sampling to determine the presence, identity, or amount of mold present
   c. Obtain any other information that the laboratory deems useful to determine the final interpretation of results

Certifications

3. In addition to the requirements for all Mold Analysis Laboratories listed in this Code (relating to licensing and/or registration and insurance requirements), Applicants must submit documentation showing that their laboratory has been licensed by the EPA and/or agent thereof to implement ERMI testing.

Fees

4. Pay the appropriate fees established by the municipality. Fees are based on a one-year license or registration.

Simple Solutions for Common Mold Problems

Once you know what to look for, and how to handle it, dealing with common mold problems may not be as difficult as you think. Here we provide some tips and solutions for some of the most common mold problems.

This part of the publication is divided into paragraphs, each pertaining to a mold-related subject. Each paragraph is numbered; therefore, paragraphs are referred to by mold-related subject and paragraph number. All cross-references are by paragraph notation.

Note: The following personal protective equipment (PPE) should be worn during the remediation process:

- A minimum of an N-95 respirator
- Gloves made from natural rubber, neoprene, nitrile, polyurethane, or PVC
- Safety glasses or goggles

Simple Solutions for Common Mold Problems—*Quick Reference Guide*

Basement Water Intrusion

1. If there are moisture intrusion issues, but no visible cracks, some possible causes for this problem include:

   - Gutter down spouts disconnected or need adjusting
   - Sump pump failure
   - Improper installation of a sump pump
   - Water table too high
   - Moisture wicking
   - Improper grade causing ground water to flow inward towards building

2. If applicable, plywood, drywall, or ceiling tiles may have to be removed for further investigation. Remove water-damaged items within 48 hours! A professional basement waterproofing and structural foundation repair expert may be needed.
3. Dehumidification is key—dry it up!

Chronic Relative Humidity Problems

4. This is common in the following circumstances:

   - Moisture entry by air leakage and vapor diffusion
   - Psychrometric properties of air
   - Excessive humidity and condensation
   - Building pressure differential
   - Vapor pressure differential

5. It's best to contact a professional HVAC contractor to solve the above problems. Additionally, consider routine use of a dehumidifier and closely monitor your moisture levels.

Clogged Window Wells

6. Window wells should be kept clean and free of leaves and debris. Make sure that the drain tile is draining properly, and not blocked with leaves, mud, etc. Pea gravel should be used and replaced yearly

so that water can freely drain and not sit up against the foundation walls. Do not use crushed stone in window wells. Additionally, it's a "best practice" not to use plastic or other non-porous materials to cover windows; these products can trap moisture and humidity, and become a breeding ground for mold and release trillions of mold spores into the building. Steel grates are a healthier option and will allow the window wells to breathe.

Damaged Coolant Line Insulation

7. If left unnoticed, improperly insulated AC coolant coil lines can drip and result in mold. Check your AC coolant coil line. You may have to use an infrared camera if the line is buried within the wall or ceiling of your building. Make sure that the AC coolant coil line is properly wrapped with the appropriate insulation to prevent leakage.

Damp Crawl Space

8. The earth's soil has very high humidity. This water vapor moves easily into crawl spaces and upward into the house environment; a damp environment is unhealthy and destructive. Mold thrives by producing airborne mold spores by the millions.
9. Consider installing a crawlspace ventilation system (similar to a radon mitigation system)—you can free your home or office of excess moisture, musty odors, dangerous gases and air pollutants that can cause structural damage and health problems. Remember, the natural airflow of your home is from the ground up through the roof. As a result, the air you breathe upstairs emanates from the crawl space. By reducing moisture and improving the air quality in your crawl space, you will breathe healthier air.
10. If cost is an issue, we recommend a crawlspace liner (1 mil. Plastic sheet) can be used to control dampness.
11. The estimated cost for a radon mitigation system is $900-$1,400 (depending on the square footage).

Duct Cleaning Services

12. We recommend a "Roto Brush" or similar technology duct cleaner. Imagine a portable shop vacuum with a soft-bristled brush attached to a spinning cable which runs inside the vacuum hose. As the duct cleaners feed the vacuum hose and brush through the air ducts, a tornado-like effect is created. The brush loosens up the dirt, hair and microorganisms, while the vacuum removes it from air ducts. The brush polishes the inner walls of the duct work to "like-new" condition. We also suggest that the HVAC system be treated with an EPA-approved antimicrobial solution after cleaning.

Excessive Humidity

13. If overall humidity levels are high, consider routine use of a dehumidifier and monitor your moisture levels closely. You may also want to purchase a hygrometer. (Cost estimate is $25-$30.) This will tell you when too much moisture is in the air. Mold grows when humidity levels surpass 60%.

Excessive Mold Spores

14. Clean! Clean! Clean! Once the mold and moisture problem has been identified and corrected, physical extraction of mold and mold spores is critical. Simply encapsulating or painting over with primer is not acceptable.
15. Commercial-grade air scrubbers should be used to remove excessive mold spores. Additionally, the home's exposed interior surfaces should be treated with an EPA-registered, anti-microbial solution to prevent future growth.
16. Consider installing ultraviolet lights or similar Furnace purifying devices. They install easily and quickly in new or existing systems. They also provide continuous cleaning of the coils and drain pans located with the furnace. Ultraviolet lights use ultraviolet energy and this energy penetrates even the tiniest microbe to disrupt its DNA structure, killing or deactivating the microorganism (fungi, mold) within seconds.

17. **<u>NOTE</u>**: Whether or not a specific type of mold is present shall not change the remediation method of removing or cleaning contaminated materials and a final surface HEPA vacuuming.

Foundation Cracks

18. If a concrete expansion joint is missing or compromised, it can cause water intrusion. Use a hydrostatic sealing caulk that can be used to seal gaps between concrete driveway, walks, patios and house foundation. This type of sealing caulk is only useful for horizontal cracks. For vertical epoxy, injection cement may be required.

19. Use a dehumidifier to reduce excessive moisture in the air. Reconnect (adjust) gutter down spouts; and re-grade planting area so that water flows away from the home.

Foundation Moisture Wicking

20. By nature, concrete is hygroscopic (readily taking up moisture). The underside of the concrete footing will transfer ground water inside the foundation, "wicking moisture," and diffusing it into the interior of the basement where excessive humidity, chronic dampness and potential mold can occur. The moisture evaporates from either face of the wall (inside and/or outside), allowing more to be drawn from below the footing. The height to which the moisture will wick is determined by the evaporation rate and type of foundation wall.

21. It's best to contact a professional foundation contractor to solve the above problems. However, again, dehumidification is the key to protecting the inside of the building. Consider routine use of a dehumidifier and monitor closely your moisture levels. Additionally, applying an antimicrobial solution to all interior wood surfaces that comes into contact with concrete is recommended.

Furnace Inspection

22. Please have furnace checked by a professional HVAC contractor.

General Indoor Air Quality Recommendations

23. The acronym MERV stands for "Minimum Efficiency Reporting Value." The MERV rating is the standard method for comparing the efficiency of an air filter. The higher the MERV rating, the better the filter is at removing particles from the air. Therefore, it's recommended that a higher MERV-rated furnace filter be used to reduce mold and microorganisms in the air.

24. **NOTE**: If indoor mold levels are greater than or equal to outdoor mold levels, microfiltration devices should be considered.

Electrostatic Furnace Filters

25. The estimated cost for simple electrostatic filters that are 1" are $179-$198 each. As a standard, indoor mold levels will typically contain only one-fourth (1/4) of the mold spores when compared to outdoor air. (Electrostatic filters will help).

Gutter and Downspouts

26. Downspouts need adjusting to ensure that water flows away from the home. It is always a good idea, however, to grade the earth away from the home and extend the downspouts 8-10' away from the foundation.

Heating, Ventilation, and Air Conditioning (HVAC) Contamination

27. For homes that have been confirmed with a moderate to high ERMI score, or molds that are infectious, do not run the HVAC system if you think it is contaminated with mold—it could spread mold throughout your home. Turn off your HVAC system and cover vents and ducts during cleaning to prevent contamination.

28. The entire HVAC system should be cleaned and free of mold. An EPA-approved disinfectant solution approved for HVAC systems shall be used to disinfect the HVAC system.

29. Dirt, debris and moisture should not be allowed to accumulate inside an HVAC unit. Additionally, air purification and micro-filtration

devices designed to disrupt microorganisms' reproduction, bind or trap mold spores and debris are acceptable.

30. **<u>NOTE</u>**: Surfaces inside the HVAC system must be completely free of mold colonies before disinfectants are applied. Remember to isolate the HVAC system; shut down the HVAC power at the main electrical box; and place critical barriers over all supply and return openings.

Ice Damming

31. Ice damming is the result of excessive attic heat. An ice dam is a ridge of ice that forms at the edge of a roof and prevents melting snow (water) from draining off the roof. The water that backs up behind the dam can leak into a home and cause damage to walls, ceilings, insulation, and other areas.

32. During the winter, keep the indoor temperature at a minimum to reduce future ice damming. Ceiling fans should be reversed to reduce warm air from rising. Additionally, consider using roof and gutter de-icing cables.

Moisture Collecting On Window Interiors

33. Most interior condensation problems are the result of poor household ventilation. By controlling your home's humidity, you can usually limit interior window condensation.

Moisture at the Bottom of the Drywall

34. Make sure that a water pipe has not burst. Then, check the exterior's downspouts to ensure that they do not need adjusting so water flows away from the home. It is always a good idea to keep as much water away from the home as possible. Properly grading the earth away and extending the downspouts 8-10' away from the foundation will help.

Moisture in Drywall Ceiling

35. First, check all plumbing stacks and exhaust flues penetrating the roof, and make sure openings are sealed. Then make sure the water pipes in that attic have not burst. Make sure gutters are cleaned and free of debris. Hire a roofing contractor to investigate any missing shingles.

Moisture Entry by Capillary Suction

36. Water, where it is in contact with a porous solid, can move through the solid due to attraction of the molecules of the liquid to those of the solid. This is common in the following circumstances:
    - Concrete slab
    - Concrete block
    - Gaps between shingled building materials

37. It is best to contact a professional foundation contractor to solve the above problems.

Moisture Intrusion

38. Unsealed gaps between construction materials, cracks in exteriors, poorly-sealed/maintained expansion joints, roof leaks, wind-driven rain, poorly sealed/maintained joints between exterior cladding and windows, doors, etc., can all create moisture intrusions problems. And, if left unnoticed, can cause mold and water damage to your property. Check often to make sure that no moisture is getting into the building. Caulking with a hydrostatic caulk is best practice. Concrete patios and walkways should be sealed with a concrete sealant and sloped away from building structure.

Moisture is Causing Wood/Finished Flooring to Buckle

39. A dehumidifier should take care of the existing moisture problem. The existing floor system may have to be removed. Use a moisture reader to determine dehumidification success.

Ozone Machines

40. If you are using a portable ozone machine(s) to control airborne contaminants, we strongly recommend that you discontinue use. The below information was found on the EPA Web Site:

41. **How is Ozone Harmful?** *Relatively low amounts can cause chest pain, coughing, shortness of breath, and throat irritation. Ozone may also worsen chronic respiratory diseases such as asthma and compromise the ability of the body to fight respiratory infections. People vary widely in their susceptibility to ozone. Healthy people, as well as those with respiratory difficulty, can experience breathing problems when exposed to ozone.*

Portable Air Cleaners

42. It's recommended that a portable air cleaner be purchased to control mold and microorganisms and other dust particles. (This unit can be placed where occupants of the home spend most of their time.)

Sewer Gas Build-Up in Homes

43. "Sewer Gas" is a mixture of gases generated by bacteria and fungi as the result of digesting wastes. Often, this gas contains methane, hydrogen sulfide ammonia, carbon dioxide, and carbon monoxide. (This is not to be confused with natural mold colonization of spores.)

44. The source of sewer gas is typically from dried out traps in drains, sumps, ejector pits, especially in floor drains of the home. This is common in homes that have been vacant for a time or have had the water turned off. It is also very common in foreclosed homes. Sewage gas is typically restricted from entering buildings through plumbing traps that create a water seal at potential points of entry. In addition, plumbing vents allow sewer gases to be exhausted outdoors. Infrequently-used plumbing fixtures may allow sewer gas to enter a home due to evaporation of water in the trap, especially in dry weather. One of the most common traps to dry out is floor drains such as those typically placed near home

furnaces and water heaters. Infrequently-used utility sinks, tubs, showers, and restrooms also are common culprits.

45. Exposure to sewer gas also can happen if the gas seeps in via a leaking plumbing drain or vent pipe, or even through cracks in a building's foundation. Sewer gas is typically denser than atmospheric gases and may accumulate in basements, and eventually mix with surrounding air.

46. Sewer gas build-up can be solved easily by using the fixtures regularly or adding water to the drains, pits etc.

Stack Effect (Positive Air)

47. This is a natural phenomenon that could affect the air you breathe. The "stack effect" occurs when warm air rises through air leaks between a home's upper floor and attic and draws outside air into the home through leaks between the floor and crawl space or basement. This happens in summer and winter and is similar to the way a chimney operates. Warm air rises because it is lighter than cold air and, since it has no place to go, it escapes from the upper levels of our homes. But when air escapes, new air has to come in to replace the escaped air. This "new air" typically comes from the crawl space vents and up from the ground, which is usually filled with moisture. As you may imagine, the quality of this replacement air is not good and may be filled with mold, mold spores, and mildew.

Keep garages, basements and crawlspaces clean and free of excessive contents and clutter.

48. The natural airflow of your home is from the ground up through the roof. As a result, the air you breathe upstairs originates from the basement or crawl space and the lower levels of the house. Therefore, it is critical to especially keep these areas clean and free from clutter that can easily get trapped and create moisture and mold.

49. By eliminating excessive contents and clutter, you will reduce the mold problem and ultimately improve your indoor air quality.

50. **There are two other recommended options:**

- Open windows for a few hours, daily; or
- Invest in a solar-powered attic fan, to insure proper house ventilation.

Skylight Leaking

51. Verify that the supposed leak is not actually excessive condensation that has moved along the underside of the glass toward the edge and then dripped down the side of the interior opening. This is most likely in very cold climates, in single-glazed skylights, and in damp locations such as bathrooms and kitchens areas.

52. Verify that the skylight is fully closed and that any weather seals are in good condition (pliable, not deformed or torn). Problems typically occur when skylights are located in very high ceilings and it's difficult to see if they are fully closed. Look carefully at the roofing or flashing on vents and other penetrations further up the roof. A leak in this area can travel quite a distance before finding its way to an indoor opening at the skylight.

Sump Pump Failure

53. Possible causes:

- GFI needs to be reset
- Fuse is blown
- No electric
- Sump pump needs to be replaced
- Auto turn-on valve needs adjusting
- Valve is set too high allowing stagnant water to collect

54. Consider replacing or adjusting the existing sump pump. Foundation water should be automatically pumped out as soon as that water pit is half full. This will prevent flooding in case of heavy rain. Also, consider a battery back-up for the system.

Tightly-Sealed Attic Spaces

55. Tightly-sealed attic spaces or overly-insulated attics are not healthy. Relative humidity can reach 100% during seasonal changes and this can cause excessive moisture and mildew/mold to form on the underside of the roof deck sheathing. If excessive humidity persists, moisture can eventually leak into a home from the attic through exhaust fans, AC returns and supplies, and even fixtures.

56. Do not vent bath exhaust fans directly into the attic space. This will cause excessive moisture and mold. Make sure insulation is not blocking soffit baffle ventilation and allow for proper ventilation for attic space. More vents may have to be added.

Visible Mold

57. Visible mold in Attic (underneath roof decking and roof joist); visible mold underneath sub-floor and floor joint; Visible mold on construction materials such as drywall, wood studs, paneling, etc.

58. Use "dry ice" blasting or an effective "mildewcide" to remove mold/mildew from these areas. A disinfection treatment with a mild, antimicrobial solution application should also include the basement, HVAC, and attic. Using dry ice blasting or mildewcide can also reduce mold and mildew staining.

59. **NOTE**: If the drywall or any other construction materials have been compromised, remove them.

Water Damage (From Leaks, High Humidity)

60. Remove all compromised construction materials within 48 hours!

61. Carpet, fabric and porous material such as upholstery, furniture, drapes, ceiling tiles and partitions, should be removed.

62. **NOTE**: Books, paper manuscripts, etc. can be professionally restored. (If non-valuable, discard.) See the Mold Remediation guidelines established by US EPA: "A Brief Guide To Mold,

Moisture, And Your Home"—EPA 402-K-02-003 and "Mold Remediation in Schools and Commercial Buildings"—EPA 402-K-01-001.

Whole-House Fan

63. This is a type of fan that is installed in a building's ceiling, and is designed to pull hot air out of the building. It is sometimes confused with an attic fan. A whole-house fan forces the hot air into the attic space. This causes a positive pressure in the attic and air is forced out through the gable and/or soffit vents. At the same time, it produces a negative pressure inside the living areas which draws cool air in through open windows. By comparison, attic fans only serve to remove some hot air; no direct cooling effect is provided to the actual living space.

64. To prevent mold spore accumulation in the living areas of the home, consider running the house fan daily for one hour.

Window and Door Leaks

65. If a window or patio door is failing, on the verge of failure, leaking, sticking or falling apart, it should be replaced.

12 Mold Prevention Tips

Your "cooling coil" (the lungs of your furnace) is a perfect breeding ground for mold, bacteria, and viruses due to condensation. While your furnace or air-conditioner is operating, it continually recirculates mold, bacteria, and viruses

Keep your furnace clean! Here are some top tips:

- Before the heating season, forced air heating systems should be inspected and, if necessary, cleaned.
- Before the cooling season, several components of the central air conditioning system should be cleaned or maintained.
- Bushes and vegetation should be trimmed around the outside condenser unit and coil and the fan should be cleaned.
- Furnace filters should be replaced or cleaned several times per season and the condensation drain should be regularly checked to ensure that it's carrying off excess moisture.
- A window-installed air conditioner has the same components as a central system, so routine maintenance of these units should include keeping the filters and coils clean. In addition, the condenser coil and intake vents should be free from obstruction and the condensation drain outlet should be kept unplugged and positioned away from the house.
- Consider installing ultraviolet lights or similar furnace purifying devices. They install easily and quickly in new or existing systems. They also provide continuous cleaning of the coils and drain pans located within the furnace. Ultraviolet lights use ultraviolet energy and this energy penetrates even the tiniest microbe to disrupt its DNA structure, killing or deactivating the microorganism (fungi, mold) within seconds.
- Keep heating, ventilation, and air conditioning (HVAC) drip or condensation pans clean and flowing properly.

Other Tips:

- Repair plumbing leaks in the building structure as soon as possible and also repair all source(s) of moisture problem(s) as soon as possible.
- Exhaust all moisture producing appliances such as bath exhaust and dryer vents to the outside. (Do not vent bath exhaust fans directly <u>into</u> the attic space. This will cause excessive moisture and mold).
- Maintain low indoor humidity, below 55% relative humidity (RH).

- Every building should have a **dehumidifier** (an electrical appliance that removes excess humidity) and should not be confused with a **humidifier.** If applicable, purchase one with an optional hose drain feature, so you do not have to worry about constantly emptying the unit. Additionally, new models have built in RH hygrometers that will automatically turn on and off when the RH reaches its desired settings.

Glossary of Common Terms

Aerobiology—The study of airborne microorganisms, pollen, spores, and seeds, esp. as agents of infection.

Affidavit—A written declaration made under oath before a notary public or other authorized officer.

Allergen—Any substance, such as pollen, mold or animal dander, which can trigger an allergic response in humans and pets.

Benign—Not dangerous or harmful

Capillary Suction—The process whereby water rises above the water table into the void spaces of a soil due to tension between the water and soil particles.

Chain of Custody—A mold laboratory form which is completed by the Licensed or Registered Mold Inspector for documentation and transfer of custody of the mold samplings directly from the inspector to the mold lab.

Dehumidification—To remove atmospheric moisture from.

Disinfections—Bleach, virucidals, fungicidal, biocides, antimicrobial solutions, etc.

DNA—A nucleic acid that carries the genetic information that is unique to every organism. DNA can be found in every cell (living or dead). For example, humans have DNA in their skin and blood cells and fungi have DNA in their spores and hyphae.

DNA Sequences—Determine individual heredity characteristics.

Dormant Mold—Mold that is inactive and awaiting future moisture and food to begin mold reproduction and growth.

Environmental Relative Moldiness Index (ERMI)—A screening tool developed by the US EPA to assist in predicting the relative "mold burden" on a giving home. The ERMI was developed by screening dust samples from 1096 homes across the United States as part of the 2006 HUD American Healthy Home Survey, and ranking these homes in an RMI (Relative Moldiness Index). The ERMI score is determined by analyzing dust samples by quantitative PCR for 36 species of mold divided into two groups. Group I is comprised of 26 species of molds commonly associated with water damage. Group II is comprised of 10 species of mold common to indoor environments. By comparing the difference in Group I and Group II molds, an ERMI score is generated which can then be compared to the nationwide RMI. (Forensic Analytical)

EPA-Approved Laboratory or its agent—A company, corporation or organization that has been licensed by the Environmental Protection Agency (EPA) to implement ERMI DNA testing: Environment Relative Moldiness Index (ERMI).

Fungus—A parasitic plant lacking chlorophyll, a rigid cell wall, leaves, true stems and roots. Reproduces by spores.

Healthy Home Specialist (HHS)—The National Environmental Health Association (NEHA), the National Center for Healthy Housing (NCHH), and the National Healthy Homes Training Center and Network (Training Center) have partnered to offer a Healthy Homes Specialist credential. This credential is designed for health and housing professionals in the public, private and non-profit sectors.

Hydrostatic—Relating to fluids at rest or under pressure.

Hyphae—Fungi usually are filamentous, with the single filaments being termed hyphae. Fungal hyphae grow and branch to make a filament network (mycelium).

Immunocompromised Individuals—A state in which a person's immune system is weakened or absent. Individuals who are immunocompromised are less capable of battling infections because of an immune response that is not properly functioning. Examples of immunocompromised people are those who have HIV or AIDS, are pregnant, or are undergoing chemotherapy or radiation therapy for cancer. Other conditions, such as certain cancers and genetic disorders, can also cause a person to become immunocompromised. Immunocompromised individuals can sometimes be prone to more serious infections and/or complications than healthy people. They are also more prone to getting opportunistic infections, which are infections that do not normally afflict healthy individuals.

Insurance Adjuster—An insurance agent who investigates personal or property damage and makes estimates that affect settlements.

Licensed or Registration—A permission granted by the municipality to engage in a business or occupation or in an activity that is considered otherwise unlawful.

Moisture Intrusion—The unwanted ingression of water into a structure from an exterior location.

Mold—Any living or dead fungi or related products or parts, including spores, hyphae, and spore-producing structures.

Mold Allergy—Human allergic reaction (such as skin rashes, open sores, and respiratory problems) from exposure to airborne mold spores and indoor mold growth.

Mold Analysis—The examination of a sample collected during a mold inspection for the purpose of determining the amount or presence of; or identifying the genus and species of any living or dead mold present in the sample.

Mold Analysis Laboratory—A company, corporation, or organization that performs mold analysis on a sample collected to determine the presence, species, identity, or amount of indoor mold in the sample

Mold Assessment—A process performed by a mold inspector that includes the physical sampling and detailed evaluation of data obtained from a building history and inspection to formulate an initial hypothesis about the origin, identity, location, and extent of amplification of mold growth of greater than 10 square feet.

Mold Inspection—An inspection, investigation, or survey of a dwelling or other structure to determine the presence of mold and excessive moisture.

Mold Inspector—A person who has been licensed or registered by the municipality to perform mold inspections.

Mold Investigation—Advanced, in depth mold inspection and mold tests to find all mold infestation inside a building.

Mold Lawyer/Mold Attorney—An environmental attorney or environmental lawyer who specializes in prosecuting or defending mold-related legal problems & lawsuits.

Mold Maintenance—Mold prevention requires effective building maintenance to prevent roof leaks, water leaks, water problems, and mold growth.

Mold Remediation—Cleaning mold from building material surfaces or the removal of contaminated building materials that are unsalvageable. Other activities, include applying disinfection procedures which are intended to prevent future mold contamination.

Mold Remediator—A person licensed or registered by the municipality to perform mold remediation.

Mold Report Results—A written presentation from a municipality-approved mold inspector to a client of the physical building inspection findings and mold sampling mold lab results, detailed analysis thereof, and recommendations for specific mold remediation and removal steps that are required to remove any mold problem documented in the report.

Mold Spore—A small reproductive cell that is resistant to unfavorable environmental conditions such as no water, and is capable of mold reproduction fungal growth when water and organic materials for consumption exist.

Mold-Contaminated Materials—Materials determined to be mold-contaminated through visual and/or olfactory inspection or other sampling methods.

Municipality—A place with its own local government (e.g., a city, town, or other area).

Olfactory—Relating to, or contributing to the sense of smell.

Opportunistic and Infectious Mold—Molds that that take advantage of certain opportunities to cause disease. Those opportunities are called "opportunistic condition." These molds are often ones that can remain dormant in body tissues for many years (e.g., the human herpes virus), or those that are extremely common but usually cause no symptoms of illness. When the immune system cannot raise an adequate response, these microorganisms are activated, begin to multiply, and can soon overwhelm the body's weakened defenses.

Ordinance—A law, statute, or regulation enacted by a Governmental Entity. An ordinance is a law passed by a municipal government.

Pathogenic—Capable of causing disease. For example, Aspergillus is a family of fungal organisms and mold, some of which can cause Aspergillosis disease.

Real-Time PCR—A DNA-based analytical method.

Scientific Basis—Regulated by or conforming to the principles of exact science.

Sick Building Syndrome—An environmentally unhealthy house or other building containing mold infestation, biological contamination, or lead paint, asbestos, radon, etc., resulting in serious health problems for its occupants.

Standardize—To cause to conform to a standard.

UVC or Ultraviolet C Lights—**Germicidal light(s) that provides continuous cleaning of the coils and drain pans located with the furnace.**

Resources

USA labs—Utilizing EPA's DNA-Based Technology
Trained Mold Inspectors
MoldDNA™ Home Mold Test Kits (Do-it-Yourself)
Visit www.MoldDNA.com

**For updated mold tips and other mold-related resources
Visit www.knowmold.com**

References

1. Wickman M, Ahlstedt S, Lilja G, van Hage Hamsten M. Quantification of IgE antibodies simplifies the classification of allergic diseases in 4-year-old children.
    A report from the prospective birth cohort study—BAMSE. Pediatr Allergy Immunol 2003;14:441-7.
2. Belanger K, Beckett W, Triche E, Bracken MB, Holford T, Ren P, et al. Symptoms of wheeze and persistent cough in the first year of life: associations with indoor allergens, air contaminants, and maternal history of asthma. Am J Epidemiol 2003;158:195-202.
3. Jaakkola JJ, Hwang BF, Jaakkola N. Home dampness and molds, parental atopy, and asthma in childhood: a six-year population-based cohort study. Environ Health Perspect 2005;113:357-61.
4. Ryan PH, LeMasters G, Biagini J, Bernstein D, Grinspun SA, Shukla R, et al. Is it traffic type, volume, or distance? Wheezing in infants living near truck and bus traffic. J Allergy Clin Immunol 2005;16:279-84.
5. Ryan PH, Lemasters GK, Biswas P, Levin L, Hu S, Lindsey M, et al. A comparison of proximity and land use regression traffic exposure models and wheezing in infants.
    Environ Health Perspect 2007;115:278-84.
6. Institute of Medicine, National Academies of Science. Damp indoor spaces and health. Washington (DC): National Academies Press; 2004.p. 355.
7. WHO Europe (World Health Organization Europe). WHO guidelines for indoor air quality: dampness and mould. Copenhagen: World health Organization; 2009.

8. Salo PM, Arbes SJ Jr, Sever M, Jaramillo R, Cohn RD, London SJ, et al. Exposure to Alternaria alternata in US homes is associated with asthma symptoms. J Allergy Clin Immunol 2006;118:892-8.
9. Agarwal R, Gupta D. Severe asthma and fungi: current evidence. Med Mycol 2011;49(suppl 1):S150-7.
10. Gent JF, Ren P, Belanger K, Triche E, Bracken MB, Holford TR, et al. Levels of household mold associated with respiratory symptoms in the first year of life in a cohort at risk for asthma. Environ Health Perspect 2002;110:A781-6.
11. Bundy KW, Gent JF, Beckett W, Bracken MB, Belanger K, Triche E, et al. Household airborne Penicillium associated with peak expiratory flow variability in asthmatic children. Ann Allergy Asthma Immunol 2009;103:26-30.
12. Rosenbaum PF, Crawford JA, Anagnost SE, Wang CJ, Hunt A, Anbar RD, et al. Indoor airborne fungi and wheeze in the first year of life among a cohort of infants at risk for asthma. J Expo Sci Environ Epidemiol 2010;20:503-15.
13. Stark PC, Celed_ on JC, Chew GL, Ryan LM, Burge HA, Muilenberg ML, et al. Fungal levels in the home and allergic rhinitis by 5 years of age. Environ Health Perspect 2005;113:1405-9.
14. Garrett MH, Rayment PR, Hooper MA, Abramson MJ, Hooper BM. Indoor airborne fungal spores, house dampness and associations with environmental factors and respiratory health in children. Clin Exp Allergy 1998;28:459-67.
15. Vesper S. Traditional mould analysis compared to a DNA-based method of mould analysis. Crit Rev Microbiol 2011;37:15-24.
16. Schmechel D, Green BJ, Blachere FM, Janotka E, Beezhold DH. Analytical bias of cross-reactive polyclonal antibodies for environmental immunoassays of Alternaria alternata. J Allergy Clin Immunol 2008;121:763-8.
17. Salo PM, Sever ML, Zeldin DC. Indoor allergens in school and day care environments. J Allergy Clin Immunol 2009;124:185-92.
18. Heinrich J. Influence of indoor factors in dwellings on the development of childhood asthma. Int J Hyg Environ Health 2011;214:1-25.
19. Haugland R, Vesper S. Identification and quantification of specific fungi and bacteria. US Patent 6 387 652. May 14, 2002.

20. Vesper SJ, McKinstry C, Haugland RA, Wymer L, Ashley P, Cox D, et al. Development of an environmental relative moldiness index for homes in the U.S. J Occup Environ Med 2007;49:829-33.
21. Reponen T, Vesper S, Levin L, Johansson E, Burkle J, Ryan P, et al. High Environmental Relative Moldiness Index during infancy as predictor of age seven asthma. Ann Allergy Asthma Immunol 2011;107:120-6.
22. LeMasters G, Wilson K, Levin L, Biagini J, Ryan PH, Lockey JE, et al. High prevalence of aeroallergen sensitization among infants of atopic parents. J Pediatr 2006; 149:505-11.
23. Miller MR, Hankinson J, Brusasco V, Burgos F, Casaburi R, Coates A, et al. ATS/ ERS Task Force. Eur Respir J 2005;26:319-38.
24. Wang X, Dockery DW, Wypij D, Gold DR, Speizer FE, Ware JH, et al. Pulmonary function growth velocity in children 6 and 18 years of age. Am Rev Respir Dis 1993;148:1502-8.
25. Crapo RO, Casaburi R, Coates AL, Enright PL, Hankinson JL, Irvin CG, et al. Guidelines for methacholine and exercise challenge testing-1999. This official statement of the American Thoracic Society was adopted by the ATS Board of Directors, July 1999. Am J Respir Crit Care Med 2000;161:309-29.
26. Cho SH, Reponen T, Bernstein DI, Olds R, Levin L, Liu X, et al. The effect of home characteristics on dust antigen concentrations and loads in homes. Sci Total Environ 2006;371:31-43.
27. Reponen T, Singh U, Schaffer C, Vesper S, Johansson E, Adhikari A, et al. Visually observed mold and moldy odor versus quantitatively measured microbial exposure in homes. Sci Tot Environ 2010; 408:5565-74.
28. Campo P, Kalra HK, Levin L, Reponen T, Olds R, Lummus ZL, et al. Influence of dog ownership and high endotoxin on wheezing and atopy during infancy. J Allergy Clin Immunol 2006;118:1271-8.
29. Iossifova Y, Reponen T, Bernstein D, Levin L, Zeigler H, Kalra H, et al. House dust (1-3)-beta-D-glucan and wheezing in infants. Allergy 2007;62:504-13.
30. Epstein TG, Bernstein DI, Levin L, Khurana Hershey GK, Ryan PH, Reponen T, et al. Opposing effects of cat and dog ownership and allergic sensitization on eczema in an atopic birth cohort. J Pediatr 2011;158:265-71.

31. Haugland RA, Brinkman NE, Vesper SJ. Evaluation of rapid DNA extraction methods for the quantitative detection of fungal cells using real time PCR analysis. J Microbiol Meth 2002;50:319-23.

32. Haugland RA, Varma M, Wymer LJ, Vesper SJ. Quantitative PCR of selected Aspergillus, Penicillium and Paecilomyces species. Sys Appl Microbiol 2004;27: 198-210.

33. Holm S. A simple sequentially rejective multiple test procedure. Scand J Stat 1979; 6:65-70.

34. Vesper S, Wakefield J, Ashley P, Cox D, Dewalt G, Friedman W. Geographic distribution of Environmental Relative Moldiness Index (ERMI) molds in U.S. homes. J Environ Public Health 2011;2011:242457.

35. Vesper SJ, McKinstry C, Yang C, Haugland RA, Kercsmar CM, Yike I, et al. Specific molds associated with asthma. J Occup Environ Med 2006;48:852-8.

36. Vesper S, McKinstry C, Haugland R, Neas L, Hudgens E, Heidenfelder B, et al. Higher Environmental Relative Moldiness Index (ERMIsm) values measured in Detroit homes of severely asthmatic children. Sci Total Environ 2008;394:192-6.

37. Vesper SJ, McKinstry C, Ashley P, Haugland RA, Yeatts K, Bradham K, et al. Quantitative PCR Analysis of molds in the dust from homes of asthmatic children in North Carolina. J Environ Monit 2007;9:826-30.

38. Mendell MJ, Mirer AG, Cheung K, Tong M, Douwes J. Respiratory and allergic health effects of dampness, mold, and dampness-related agents: a review of the epidemiologic evidence. Environ Health Perspect 2011;119:748-56.

39. Meklin T, Haugland RA, Reponen T, Varma M, Lummus Z, Bernstein D, et al. Quantititive PCR analysis of house dust can reveal abnormal mold conditions. J Environ Monit 2004;6:615-20.

40. Reponen T, Singh U, Schaffer C, Vesper S, Johansson E, Adhikari A, et al. Visually observed mold and moldy odor versus quantitatively measured microbial exposure in homes. Sci Total Environ 2010; 408:5565-74.

41. Vesper S, McKinstry C, Cox D, Dewalt G. Correlation between ERMI values and other moisture and mold assessments of homes in the American Healthy Homes Survey. J Urban Health 2009;86:850-60.

42. Kercsmar CM, Dearborn DG, Schluchter M, Xue L, Kirchner HL, Sobolewski J, et al. Reduction in asthma morbidity in children as a result of home remediation aimed at moisture sources. Environ Health Perspect 2006;114:1574-80.
43. Cohen J. Statistical power analysis for the behavioral sciences. 2nd ed. Hillsdale (NJ): Lawrence Erlbaum; 1988.
44. E2. Hyvärinen A, Roponen M, Tiittanen P, Laitinen S, Nevalainen A, Pekkanen J.
45. Dust sampling methods for endotoxin—an essential, but underestimated issue. Indoor Air 2006; 15:20-7.
46. E3. Crawford C, Reponen T, Lee T, Iossifova Y, Levin L, Adhikari A, et al. Temporal and spatial variation of indoor and outdoor airborne fungal spores, pollen, and (1/3)-b-D-glucan. Aerobiologia 2009; 25:147-58
47. From the Departments of Environmental Health and Internal Medicine, University of Cincinnati; the Environmental Protection Agency, Cincinnati; and the Cincinnati Children's Hospital Medical Center. Infant origins of childhood asthma associated with specific molds—2012 American Academy of allergy, Asthma & Immunology.

Appendix "A" (1 of 1)

MoldDNA™ Report

Fungal Analysis by DNA

Midwest Aerobiology Labs Corp.
Attention: Darryl Morris
Gottlieb Memorial Hospital
675 North Ave. Suite 310
Melrose Park, IL 60160

Dust samples were collected by vacuuming 2m in bedrooms plus 2m in living rooms using Duststream sampler. Samples are analyzed using USEPA - ERMI Protocol.

Date Received: 09/04/12

Sample Location: Master / Living

Job ID | Site: 202 Tuscany, Romeoville, Illinois

Molds associated with water-damage. (Foreclosure or vacant property, flooded basements or crawlspaces, hidden moisture intrusions etc.)

Molds that are common in homes. Presence in indoor air generally reflects outside ventilation air ventilation (blown in from the outside); windows, doors etc.

Group 1

Organism	Sp Eq	Sp Eq/mg dust	%	Log Conc
Aspergillus flavus	10700	2,100	13.6	3.32
Aspergillus fumigatus	344	67	0.4	1.82
Aspergillus niger	309	61	0.4	1.78
Aspergillus ochraceus	ND	ND	-	-
Aspergillus penicilloides	9550	1,900	12.1	3.27
Aspergillus restrictus	ND	ND	-	-
Aspergillus sclerotiorum	ND	ND	-	-
Aspergillus sydowii	ND	ND	-	-
Aspergillus unguis	107	21	0.1	1.32
Aspergillus versicolor	4390	860	5.6	2.93
Aureobasidium pullulans	373	73	0.5	1.86
Chaetomium globosum	311	61	0.4	1.78
Cladosporium sphaerospermum	700	140	0.9	2.14
Eurotium amstelodami	338	66	0.4	1.81
Paecilomyces varioti	61	12	0.1	1.07
Penicillium brevicompactum	ND	ND	-	-
Penicillium corylophilum	108	21	0.1	1.32
Penicillium crustosum	ND	ND	-	-
Penicillium purpurogenum	ND	ND	-	-
Penicillium spinulosum	ND	ND	-	-
Penicillium variabile	ND	ND	-	-
Scopulariopsis brevicaulis	171	34	0.2	1.53
Scopulariopsis chartarum	29	6	-	0.75
Stachybotrys chartarum	9190	1,800	11.7	3.26
Trichoderma viride	ND	ND	-	-
Wallemia sebi	153	30	0.2	1.47
Total for Both Groups	78,684	15,000		
Sum of Logs				31.42
LOD				0.4

GROUP 1 SCORE

Group 2

Organism	Sp Eq	Sp Eq/mg dust	%	Log Conc
Acremonium strictum	1650	320	2.1	2.5
Alternaria alternata	1650	320	2.1	2.5
Aspergillus ustus	60	12	0.1	1.07
Cladosporium cladosporioides I	4880	950	6.2	2.97
Cladosporium cladosporioides II	456	89	0.6	1.94
Cladosporium herbarum	647	130	0.8	2.11
Epicoccum nigrum	31900	6,300	40.6	3.79
Mucor racemosus	60	12	0.1	1.07
Penicillium chrysogenum	561	110	0.7	2.04
Rhizopus stolonifer	6	1	-	0.07
Total for Both Groups	78,684	15,000		
Sum of Logs				20.06
LOD				0.4

Subtract Group 2 from Group 1 to get ERMI Score

GROUP 2 SCORE

ERMI Score

GROUP 1 — 31.42
GROUP 2 — = 20.06

ERMI SCORE = 11.4

LEVEL — Risk Level → Level 4

ERMI Score	Level or Risk	Likelihood of Mold Problem in Home
-10 to -4	Level 1	Lowest
-4 to 0	Level 2	Lower
0 to 5	Level 3	Moderate
5 to 20	Level 4	High

NOTE: Data represent only a portion of an overall IAQ investigation. Visual information and environmental conditions measured during the site assessment (humidity, moisture readings, etc.) are crucial to any final interpretation of the results.